Praise for *Unwrapped*

The Christmas season can be difficult to navigate and isn't always the joy-filled celebration it's made out to be. In this must-read book, Dr. Cassie Reid shares practical ways to overcome past hurts, family baggage, negative emotions, and many other dynamics in order to bring peace and fun back into the holidays.

—Pastor Jimmy Evans
Founder & CEO MarriageToday

Dr. Reid's book will save your sanity during Christmas by inspiring you to reach for your faith and recognize how to live it out during the blessed season. Filled with personal recollections, *Unwrapped* will pull on your heartstrings until you give in to the joy of the season by seeing those around you differently. This is the perfect book for anyone wanting to get through the holidays in one piece and enjoy it along the way.

—Linda Metcalf, PhD
Director of Graduate Counseling Programs
Texas Wesleyan University

Cassie has a unique perspective on building close relationships and handling the stress of family dynamics during special occasions. In her easy-to-read book, *Unwrapped*, she gives practical advice that will help you begin enjoying the holidays instead of merely enduring them. This is required reading if you want to learn how to make lasting happy memories with your family during times of celebration.

—Amie Stockstill
Founder
Echo (Training for Women Communicators)

Dr. Reid's honest insights into managing expectations (including disappointments) during what can be an extremely stressful time for many families are invaluable. *Unwrapped* is essential for anyone looking for some support during the holidays!

—Sally L. Pretorius
Family Law Attorney
Koons Fuller Law

Cassie is brilliantly honest about herself and the truth around the Christmas tree. I love transparent people who are willing to say they have *unaccomplishments* and share what they have learned on their journey. This book is personal, solid, and applicable. Much more than a survival kit, it's a perspective-changer.

—Lisa Jennett
Author of *When I Last Saw Me*

Dr. Reid has written a vital spiritual book for anyone wanting to dive into the true internal feelings associated with the holiday season. Read this book and learn from one of the best.

—Marcene Weatherall
Intervention Counseling Coordinator
Keller Independent School District

This is one of the most impactful books for restoring sanity to the holidays (or any family event). You'll want to keep it within arm's reach as a reference source for navigating your heart through the holidays.

—Glenna Massey
Healing Place Pastor Cross Timbers Church

UNWRAPPED

OPEN THE GIFT OF HOLIDAY SANITY

UNWRAPPED

OPEN THE GIFT OF HOLIDAY SANITY

CASSIE REID, PHD, LCP-S

 GATEWAY® PRESS

TKU ✠ PRESS

ISBN: 978-1-945529-90-0 Paperback
ISBN: 978-1-945529-91-7 eBook

We hope you hear from the Holy Spirit and receive God's richest blessings from this book by Gateway Press and TKU Press. We want to provide the highest quality resources that take the messages, music, and media of Gateway Church to the world. For more information on other resources from Gateway Publishing, go to gatewaypublishing.com.

Gateway Press, an imprint of Gateway Publishing
700 Blessed Way
Southlake, TX 76092
gatewaypublishing.com

Printed in the United States of America
18 19 20 21 22   5 4 3 2 1

To all the individuals who have trusted me enough to let me into their world, especially James. I consider it an honor.

In Him was life, and the life was the light of men. And the light shines in the darkness, and the darkness did not comprehend it.

—John 1:4-5 NKJV

Then the Grinch thought of something he hadn't before! "What if Christmas," he thought, "doesn't come from a store. What if Christmas . . . perhaps . . . means a little bit more!"

—Dr. Seuss, *How the Grinch Stole Christmas*

TABLE OF CONTENTS

FOREWORD

When Cassie Reid asked me to write the foreword to her book, I felt a bit unworthy. After all, I am a worship leader, and she is a psychologist who has more education in her little finger than I have in my whole body! Then I realized that what Cassie feels kindred about our friendship is the purity of capture and release. Worship music has always played a big part in her road to freedom. It is the thread God often uses to sew our hearts back together as we release the pain and fear He never intended for us to carry.

Cassie may be the smartest friend I've ever had. Her depth and understanding, along with her skill and knowledge, have always put her on a pedestal as my "super smart friend." Yet my favorite thing about Cassie is not her education nor her successful career. My favorite thing about her is that she's real! Cassie is down-to-earth and willing to acknowledge and tackle her own fears. She is not only aware of her progress but also of the need to continue her journey to fuller freedom.

Cassie's practical approach to growth is enhanced by her prophetic nature. Her desire to recognize God's presence in the wreckage of life as well as in the healing He offers to all of us is inspiring! Life is a continuous learning curve, and every day we have the opportunity to grow or shrink back. Cassie faithfully stewards her calling to bring others into a safe place, trading deferred hope for a longing fulfilled. Her determination in walking weary souls into wholeness is lathered in kindness and caution. She understands and respects the way the heart bends in grief and sorrow and has learned the art of encouraging it to stand tall again.

I hope you will capture these gifts in Cassie as you read *Unwrapped*. I sincerely believe this book will bring fresh healing and joy to every person who is willing to embrace her words that have been so carefully crafted and covered in prayer. Cassie is a gift to the world, and I'm so proud to call her my friend.

Rita Springer
Worship Leader, Songwriter, and Artist

ACKNOWLEDGMENTS

I first want to thank my husband, James, who showed me that the holidays can be about more than disappointment and lack. They can be about blessing and joy too. Thank you for believing in me when I didn't believe in myself, for seeing the diamonds in the rough, and for knowing that there is more to me than what I see.

I also want to thank my girls, Londi and Emerson. You show me true joy in the season (and throughout the year) and have allowed me to redeem so many memories through the way you see things.

Thank you to my immediate family. This book is also for you—a sign of my commitment to allow the Holy Spirit to speak to and through me, creating new memories and redeeming the old.

To my iron: Lisa, Stacy, Rita, Michelle, Mari, Amie, and many others: You have allowed me the space to explore what is within me without judgment or restrictions. You have encouraged me and pushed me forward in seasons when I needed it the most. Thank you for sharpening me.

To the stellar Gateway Publishing team:

- Thank you, Craig, for your leadership and wisdom. Thank you for allowing this message to find a space on the shelves.
- Thank you, John, for looking beyond the words and seeing my random thoughts as something more. You have such great vision.

- Thank you, Kathy, Jenny, Peyton, James, Caleb, and Cady, for being so patient, kind, and lovely. You are always such a joy.

To Gabbi: You are a creative genius. I am still so in shock that you would create something on my behalf. Thank you!

Thank you to Gateway Church where I have been able to discover more about myself, do things with excellence, and speak what the Holy Spirit has placed on my heart. I am forever grateful to Pastor Debbie Morris, Pastor Lynda Grove, Pastor Mallory Bassham, Pastor Jan Greenwood, and the many others who saw something in me and made space for it to be developed.

Thank you to Dr. Becky Taylor, Dr. Linda Metcalf, Dr. Glen Jennings, and Dr. Rebecca Fredrickson. You helped me develop my gift and gain my education, and you didn't try to change what the Holy Spirit put within me. This is phenomenal in a field where finding room to hear the Holy Spirit is obsolete. I am grateful for your leadership, the trails you blazed so I can walk forward, and the kindness you showed along the way. You have made room for me to become who I am today.

Lastly, I want to thank you—yes, *you*! I am so honored that you would trust me enough to read these words. You have let me into a piece of your world, and I am always honored when folks do that. It is a privilege, and I take the responsibility very seriously. Thank you for reading these words and for the bravery it takes to implement them.

INTRODUCTION

Many people experience the complete opposite of joy, peace, and fun during the Christmas season. Some individuals seem to be incredibly blessed, as though their lives are the plot of a romantic Christmas movie. If we looked a little closer, though, I suspect we would see some cracks in that perfect facade. Most of us probably live somewhere in the middle. We experience this time of year with a mixture of joy, fun, and yes, disappointment.

This little book sprung out of my own struggles with the Christmas season. Yes, I also come from a *family*, so you know what I mean. I started writing after a personally horrible holiday. I simply needed to vent, so I sat at my computer and typed out my thoughts. Before long, a pattern emerged, and a book came together. I don't normally recommend writing this way; it's just what happened. At first, I surprised myself. I didn't realize I had so much to process, especially since I spend a good deal of time analyzing my experiences and trusting the Holy Spirit to do the rest of the work. As I continued writing, I realized I still had so many emotions, reactions, and thoughts about the Christmas holiday swirling around inside me.

Before you read any further, I must tell you that the theme of these chapters is TBH ("to be honest"). I understand many people, including myself, accept internal dishonesty, which prevents all of us from living our best possible lives. So I encourage you to be honest about your experiences, both past and present.

I will do my best to do the same. Otherwise, we will rob ourselves of the freedom God intends for us. Give the Holy Spirit room to speak to you and connect with the hurt places inside you. Only then will you find true peace.

My life's mission is to use my story and experiences to help others process their own stories, all with the help of the Holy Spirit. I sincerely pray you will do just that as you read this book. And I pray the thoughts I share here will give you hope, courage, and gumption:

- **Hope** to see you can experience change
- **Courage** to face the truth and name it
- **Gumption** to do and say what has always needed to be done and said

DISAPPOINTMENT

Meanwhile, the moment we get tired in the waiting, God's Spirit is right alongside helping us along. If we don't know how or what to pray, it doesn't matter. He does our praying in and for us, making prayer out of our wordless sighs, our aching groans. He knows us far better than we know ourselves, knows our pregnant condition, and keeps us present before God. That's why we can be so sure that every detail in our lives of love for God is worked into something good.

—Romans 8:26–28 MSG

I believe one word sums up the negative feelings many people experience during the Christmas season—**disappointment**. A family may gather around a lush tree, sip hot cocoa, and open exquisitely wrapped presents for days. But I have never found even one family to be exempt from difficulty or conflict, especially during the holidays. Still, most of us carry a picture in our minds of a mythical perfect family, with whom we compare our own less-than-perfect relatives. Many of us imagine the details of family gatherings before we even arrive. We mentally rehearse the scenarios and conversations and fanaticize about the ease of our interactions. Only minutes after our actual arrival, we are disappointed to find these expectations lying in a heap of mental rubble as all sorts of unpleasant emotions begin welling up inside us.

Most people understand disappointment as *unhappiness stemming from the failure of something hoped for or expected to happen.* As I examine this definition, though, two glaring problems arise:

- First, I must address the concept of *happiness and unhappiness.* Contemporary culture, especially within the confines of the Church, teaches that we should always do what we can to remain happy and avoid those things that make us unhappy. Consequently, many people learn to suppress their feelings and "press past" any negative emotions. However, what would happen if we learned to *lean in* rather than *press past*? We would have a healthier society if we gave individuals space to express their unhappiness, disappointments, and other negative emotions before they took root. The seeds of these negative emotions have the potential to grow bigger, uglier, and far more detrimental if left unaddressed. Whether our sister came to the house empty-handed again or our father insulted us for the 100th time in the past month alone, we need a place to express disappointment.

- Second, the word *failure* is problematic. We determine our own definitions for success, and anything that falls short is counted as a failure. This supposed failure leads to disappointment and sometimes even the belief that *we* are failures. We think if something isn't a 100% success, then it is a 100% failure. Typically, most of us experience failure by taking it as our own rather than blaming someone else. The problem with this thinking is readily apparent. Sometimes people aren't nice, and sometimes they let us down. And sometimes people are not who we thought they were or want them to be.

We would have a healthier society
if we gave individuals space to express
their unhappiness, disappointments,
and other negative emotions before
they took root.

How can you respond to disappointment?

- *Lean into the disappointment and name what or who was disappointing.*
- Let yourself *feel* it. Allow yourself the time to acknowledge that you are disappointed. You don't need to stay in that place but give yourself the grace to feel what needs to be felt.
- *Decide how you will address those feelings.*
- Many times, we take on the responsibility for the disappointment rather than allow ourselves to tell the person who disappointed us about our feelings. The enemy wants us to believe the lie that if we allow ourselves to confront disappointment, we are opening ourselves to a greater risk. This thinking leads families to sweep problems under the rug until the rug looks like a mountain in the middle of the living room.
- *Don't get stuck in disappointment.*

Lean in, take action, and move on.

We all have been disappointed. The key is to allow ourselves to lean into the emotion, find our successes, and then embrace joy.

ASSUMPTIONS

Don't assume that you know it all.
Run to God! Run from evil!
Your body will glow with health,
your very bones will vibrate with life!

—Proverbs 3:7–8 MSG

You know what they say about assumptions... don't finish that sentence! It's still true, though.

An **assumption** is *something accepted as true or as certain to happen, without proof.* Isn't that what we often do when we think about other people or upcoming events? We make an assumption or imagine the *why* without any solid, verifiable proof of its validity. This kind of thinking is like a fragile, shaky foundation. If a builder has a smooth, level, and solid surface, almost any kind of building can be constructed on top of it. Because of its stable foundation, the building will be sturdy, strong, and lasting. On the other hand, if the foundation is bumpy and uneven, then any building put on it will be wobbly, weak, and temporary. We can visualize a building, but what about thinking in terms of our relationships? How often do we allow faulty assumptions about other people and their motives to become the foundation on which we attempt to build our relationships?

Consider the following example: Your Aunt Mildred suddenly announces she can't come to the Christmas dinner you have been planning for approximately 343 days. She doesn't give a reason, or perhaps you don't particularly like the one she's given. In her absence, you choose to make the assumption that she doesn't want to be around you or your family. She doesn't like your cooking. She must even hate your dog. These thoughts take over your mind, along with many negative emotions. Now consider this: all of these thoughts are assumptions. You have taken some beliefs and accepted them as facts without any proof. Imagine the foundation you have laid with these assumptions. How do you think they will influence your next interaction with Aunt Mildred? Now you find it difficult to have an authentic conversation or interaction because your relational foundation with your aunt has become unsteady. This new situation is all due to the assumptions you made about her Christmas dinner absence. Poor Aunt Mildred! These assumptions will have an adverse effect on your future interactions with her. You have built a new relationship with her based on a foundation of uninformed judgment rather than truth.

When we make assumptions, we are actually judging other people's motives. And when we begin judging, we move into dangerous territory. In *How to Stop the Pain*, Dr. James Richards writes, "Nothing that happens outside of you has the power to hurt you *until you judge it*."[1] This quote gets me every time. Let's go back to your Aunt Mildred. Nothing about her absence has the power to hurt you *until* you start making assumptions (aka judgments) about why she isn't coming to dinner. We

---

1. James B. Richards, *How to Stop the Pain* (New Kensington, PA: Whitaker House, 2001), 24.

When we make assumptions,
we are actually judging
other people's motives.

do the work of the enemy when we allow him to plant one little assumption with which we then run.

How can you overcome the tendency to make assumptions?

- *Stop assuming!*

  Ask questions, open a dialogue, and start communicating. Then you will have room for facts rather than your own calculated fictions.
- *Ask the Holy Spirit to show you if you have made assumptions or judgments that have harmed your relationships.*

  Do you believe something about someone in your family based on what you thought rather than known facts?
- *Believe the best.*

  If we make every effort to believe those around us have good motives, we then have the capability to love them. We also have the opportunity to build solid and more permanent foundations for our relationships. I personally prefer strong, sure relationships built on facts over unsure relationships built on fabricated assumptions.

BOUNDARIES

God's name is a place of protection—
good people can run there and be safe.

—Proverbs 18:10 MSG

I know many people who have read books about setting **boundaries**. However, reading something and putting it into action are two separate things. Here's something to consider: *a boundary isn't a boundary until it's communicated.* I often encounter individuals who think they have set boundaries with other people, especially family members, but those other people have no idea anything at all has changed. They have no awareness of a set boundary. Instead, they think the supposed boundary setters are being mean or behaving in unexplainable ways. If we want to have healthy boundaries, then we are going to have to communicate them.

Here are a few helpful items to consider. I've collected these nuggets over several years as I've listened to many people tell their stories and tried to help them set boundaries.

- *The Holy Spirit needs to lead in your boundary setting; otherwise, you are only projecting your self-will on other people and situations.*

I have encountered many people who attempt to mask control in the package of a boundary.

- They want to manipulate others into doing something they want them to do.
- They want to avoid an unpleasant situation.
- They want to get their way.
- They want to avoid working on their own wounds.

This list could go on. If the Holy Spirit doesn't direct the boundary, it can lead to abuse, especially when it isn't communicated. Notice I use a serious word here: *abuse*. Many people hear this word and think about bruises or inappropriate touching. However, I have encountered many abuse victims who have never been touched by a human hand. Their experiences of abuse stem from the words and actions of others. They have been beaten up in ways that leave marks more difficult to heal than those requiring ice packs. To be clear, I have physical abuse in my own story; I am not saying it doesn't cause severe damage. It surely does, but it isn't the only way to cause great harm.

- *Just like everything else in your life, ask the Holy Spirit if He wants you to set a boundary.*

The Holy Spirit must lead; otherwise, we are pursuing our own agendas, which could keep us from experiencing His agenda. People often use the term "boundaries" as a way to protect themselves from experiencing "opportunities" to feel things they may not like to feel. I call them "opportunities" because many people throw up an arbitrary "boundary" so they don't have to feel something they dislike. Many times, when we feel something we dislike, it means we are about to conquer that very thing. We are able to take charge rather than letting that experience take charge of us. We can face what we thought was impossible and step into what is actually possible. Make sure the boundary you set is truly one He intends for you; otherwise, you will likely miss an opportunity to rise to another level.

- *Understand the "why" behind the boundary so you can set it in a healthy way.*

Typically, we have a reason for wanting to set a boundary, but sometimes people want a boundary without considering the reason for its necessity in the first place. If we harbor resentment, anger, bitterness, or regret, we will set a boundary controlled by these emotions. Whenever we allow these emotions to drive our decisions, we almost always end up with a collision. Resentment, anger, bitterness, and regret are never good reasons to set a boundary. We need to contend with these emotions rather than letting them drive our reasoning. The desire to live our best life should drive us to be authentic and live in complete freedom. Those are the right reasons to set boundaries.

- *Set boundaries in love; otherwise, you can easily turn them into ungodly weapons.*

I've seen many individuals throw up boundaries in an attempt to change another person. You can imagine how this tactic usually turns out. It's okay to want others to modify their behavior, but using a boundary as a means to do so usually causes harm and seldom gets us what we want. We might think the other person will suffer because of our firm decision. While an outcome such as this is occasionally possible, the other individual ultimately remains untouched. Now we have a boundary, but the person continues behaving the same way, and we find ourselves wounded all over again.

- *Don't use boundaries to gain a desired outcome in a situation—that is just manipulation.*

  I've already alluded to this point, but we are practicing manipulation if we construct boundaries because we expect other people to go where we want them to go and do what we want them to do. They will likely take alternative routes to hurt us anyway because we don't have the right motive for our boundaries. Even more, we don't have the right heart condition. Then two unhealthy individuals act as if they are healthy but harm each other in the process. Give your heart a check-up, which will ultimately allow you to set a boundary in the power of your authentic self.

Pray something like this:

Holy Spirit, please show me when You want me to set a boundary. Prevent me from setting a boundary only to protect myself from something You really want me to experience. Please examine my heart; I want my agenda to be Your agenda. Help me set boundaries that always heal and never wound. Show me what You want to accomplish through boundaries so that I may follow You guidance with all my heart. In Jesus name, Amen.

We are practicing manipulation if we construct boundaries because we expect other people to go where we want them to go and do what we want them to do.

CONTROL

No one can control the wind or lock it in a box.
No one has any say-so regarding the day of death.
No one can stop a battle in its tracks.
No one who does evil can be saved by evil.

—Ecclesiastes 8:8 MSG

Why does it always have to be about **control**? Control is the root of much of the push and pull we experience during the Christmas season. I confess—I have done it too. I try to control situations by setting up the ideal order to gain the optimal outcome. For example, I was supposed to go to a family party. I thought about how the planners might construct everything in such a way that it would not be possible for me to attend. Then everyone could say I was "that family member." I would be the one who was always "too busy," "too important," or "too good" for family gatherings. I don't feel any of those things, but I fear others may perceive me this way if I can't make a particular time, date, or location. Consequently, I will go into my usual pattern of trying to take care of everyone so no one will reject me. That is my fear—rejection.

As I reflected on my behavior, I realized I try to gain an optimal outcome so I can make everyone happy, I can attend, and no one will be disappointed. And I realized I like it *my way*. I like being able to manage my anxiety by managing my circumstances. But in reality, this is selfish. My intention may be good, but my motives are ultimately self-serving, regardless of how authentic the threat of rejection is to me.

The key to correcting my motives is to recognize the real root of my anxiety. What benefit do I get by controlling the outcome? What do I fear will happen if I don't? What is my true motive for enforcing the rules of my game, even when the other players are unwitting or unwilling? I have expended a lot of frivolous effort to control a fear rooted in a previous wound, but all this effort does is allow the wound to continue damaging me. This behavior is neither good nor healthy. It isn't fair to anyone else, and it certainly isn't God's best for me and those around me.

What can you do when you realize your need for control has become uncontrollable?

- *Identify the fear.*
  Figure out what causes the fear so you can eliminate the source. Is it a lie? Is it a past event that created a wound? Is it a pattern in your family system? Once you find it, you can eliminate it from your life.
- *Face the fear.*
  Something powerful happens as you look the thing you fear in the face and go to the end of it. When you take the worst-case scenario all the way to the end of the track, you realize you didn't die as a consequence. You made it. It wasn't as awful as the enemy would have you believe. Kick him out of your thoughts.
- *Figure out how you want the scenario to look.*
  You can let go of control and start embracing the moment. You don't have to fear what the moment may do to you. You can actually live your life. Isn't that what it's all about anyway?

I like being able to manage my anxiety by managing my circumstances.
But in reality, this is selfish.

EXPECTATIONS

When they see me waiting, expecting your Word,
those who fear you will take heart and be glad.

—Psalm 119:74 MSG

Another culprit seems to lurk around during the Christmas holidays—**expectations**. One of the most interesting features of expectations is that many people *never communicate them*. This movie plays in our minds—a theater with only one seat and no ticket booth. Even worse, we think everyone else has already seen the show! I am as guilty of this as anyone else. I will direct the "perfect" scene in my head and expect all the actors to take their places and follow my script. Fast forward to the credits because you already know how this movie ends. That's right, with feelings of disappointment, rejection, abandonment, and a host of other trigger responses we've been conditioned to produce.

How can you address expectations?

- *Communicate!*
  Allow the people in your life, especially those closest to you, to purchase a ticket to the movie in your mind. And once they're seated, hand them a script. Only then will they know what you expect.

- *Check those expectations.*

  Are your expectations realistic? Are they even possible? Anywhere on planet Earth? I put the last one here for my benefit. I have learned a host of new lessons through parenting a toddler. My husband and I will plan an amazing trip to see Christmas lights, but instead of enjoying the lit-up Santas and electronic holiday cheer, our daughter screams in the back seat for more crackers and fruit snacks (don't judge!). We have to make sure our expectations are even reasonable. Don't be caught elevating expectations over fun, peace, and the simple ability to enjoy the season. Take a good look at your expectations and make sure they come from pure motives rather than past hurts.

- *Give lots of grace.*

  Give grace to yourself and to everyone else around you. Allow yourself to make mistakes; everything does *not* have to be perfect. Allow others to mess up their "lines." I always laugh the hardest when improvisational comedians break character and make themselves laugh. It's contagious. Could seeing you laugh off mistakes or tensions be what your family needs this Christmas? Give them a little grace to make it through this season themselves.

I'm sincerely praying you will be able to set some realistic expectations, communicate them, and have your show go on without a hitch. Break a leg!

Don't be caught elevating expectations over fun, peace, and the simple ability to enjoy the season.

MENTAL GYMNASTICS

Worry weighs us down;
a cheerful word picks us up.

—Proverbs 12:25 MSG

Mental gymnastics. I think if my husband, James, were to describe me at the Christmas season, he would definitely use this term in the description. I don't know what it is about this time of year, but I find myself mentally constructing scenario after scenario in an attempt to discover the best one. I play out how I want things to happen, how people will feel, how we can squeeze the last drop out of a shopping trip, or how we can have the right experience at a holiday party.

In this game, I never get a perfect score. I expect my efforts to wow the "judges" and create the perfect routine, but I ultimately end up disappointed and exhausted from the struggle. Who are these judges anyway? I've never gotten a satisfactory answer to that question. The most critical, hard-to-please judge is me. I would never give myself a 10. I wear myself out trying to reach a standard I think others expect but is really just my own self-imposed burden.

Considerable research has gone into confirming that women always strive for perfection and beat themselves up when they fall short. It's probably a waste of

I wear myself out trying
to reach a standard I think others
expect but is really just my own
self-imposed burden.

research dollars. Ask any five of us, and you'll know the results. Deep down, we know perfection is impossible, but that doesn't stop us from bending over backward trying to achieve it.

How do you overcome the tendency toward mental gymnastics?

- *Recognize when you are starting your routine—your mental gymnastics.* Becoming aware is critical. If you can identify when you start these scenarios, it will bring you closer to the reasons for them. Identify when you "hit the mat."
- *Ask yourself, "Why am I doing this?"* What is it about this event or situation that makes you feel as though you must play out these scenarios? Who will be present and make you feel as though you have to perform? What makes you feel like you have to earn a perfect 10?
- *Make a change.* Ask yourself the most difficult question: "What is the purpose of this event or situation?" Now lean into the purpose. If the event is a birthday party, think about the best way to celebrate that person. If it is a Christmas party, think about how you can celebrate the season in the most fun way. You will be the one who determines the score. If you lean into the purpose, you will always score a perfect 10.

RUTS

For my part, I am going to boast about nothing but the Cross of our Master, Jesus Christ. Because of that Cross, I have been crucified in relation to the world, set free from the stifling atmosphere of pleasing others and fitting into the little patterns that they dictate. Can't you see the central issue in all this? It is not what you and I do—submit to circumcision, reject circumcision. It is what *God* is doing, and he is creating something totally new, a free life! All who walk by this standard are the true Israel of God—his chosen people. Peace and mercy on them!

—Galatians 6:14–16 MSG

Ruts. This word makes me think of farm roads. Farmers have to make their own ways through their fields to get their work done. Over time, their routes become ruts, which eventually become "roads"—as much a part of the farm as the planned roads. Over time, these ruts smooth out. When farmers need to plant or place livestock onto another parcel of land, they establish new bumpy, uncomfortable "roads."

I hope you understand my farm metaphor—I'm really talking about you and me. We create patterns in our relationships with family and friends. These patterns can eventually become "ruts." We establish norms based on our usually traveled routes. These "roads" seem easy, smooth, and comfortable because we've done things that way for quite some time. However, ruts come with their own problems; they aren't always good for us. They look like shortcuts, but sometimes we are simply repeating maladaptive behaviors.

I have seen many families whose members don't speak directly to each other about difficult issues. Instead, they share their feelings and frustrations with another family member who was not involved in the conflict. Then the newly informed person speaks to the offending family member about the issue. Why do families use this complicated go-between tactic instead of dealing with problems head-on? In my experience, it is because people see confrontation as an overwhelming risk. Individual family members are often too anxious to confront the person themselves, so they bring someone else into the situation to alleviate their anxiety. Two people in communication make a straight line, but the addition of a third person creates a triangle. In a clinical setting, we call this *triangulation*.

How can you address the ruts in your life?

- *Ask yourself and the Holy Spirit what ruts exist in your family system.*
  What patterns have gone on for some time? What maladaptive "shortcuts" have you been taking to avoid real issues? A simple acknowledgement of these behaviors for yourself will make your holiday (and many other days) go more smoothly.
- *Ask yourself and the Holy Spirit how to drive new roads.*
  What can you do differently that will allow others around you not to fall into old patterns? What alternative routes can you take that will allow you to operate at another level of freedom? When you drive new roads, you might find yourself a bit uncomfortable at first, but they will get you where you

They look like shortcuts,
but sometimes we are simply
repeating maladaptive behaviors.

want to go. You will establish a new way of doing things. Ultimately, you may discover new roads your entire family can use in the future.

- *Ask yourself and the Holy Spirit why the ruts in your family were established in the first place.*

This exploration is helpful because it will let you see *why*. Discovering the reasons for the ruts will give you grace and understanding and bring change to your family's life.

TWO-FOR-ONE

And this is why a man leaves father and mother and cherishes his wife. No longer two, they become "one flesh."

—Ephesians 5:31 MSG

You may wonder why I am discussing marriage during the Christmas season. Really, it is quite relevant. Many families forget about the concept of marriage when it comes to holiday gatherings. This may seem like a strong statement, but untold numbers of families welcome their own members warmly but then give a big dose of rejection to one or more spouses. That is why I call this concept **two-for-one**. Jesus reminded His followers that two become one when a couple marries (Mark 10:8). So why do families still try to separate the union of couples in their own families for their own benefits?

I recently had the privilege of working with a couple preparing for marriage. Both the man and the woman had heard the Lord and felt as if marriage was the right thing to do. However, the man's family—his parents specifically—disagreed. The holidays occurred during our time together, and I found it fascinating (i.e., horrifying) how those parents alienated the spouse-to-be while embracing their own son.

31

The deliberate difference in how his parents treated the two members of this couple was shocking, especially at a time of year that is supposed to encourage unity.

I experienced something similar firsthand. My sister was dating a young man, and my family—myself included—did not approve. My husband and I spoke out against the relationship because, at the time, the young man wasn't treating her very well. We voiced our opinion with the good intention of protecting my sister and trying to help her see her worth. Our words were powerful, though. Fast forward many years, and my sister chose to marry him in spite of the family's objections. It was a difficult and uncomfortable time because we had wounded both of them so significantly. When the time for the wedding arrived, they begrudgingly extended us an invitation. Today, this brother-in-law is one of our favorite family members. He willingly admits he wasn't the most mature person during his early relationship with my sister, but he loves her, and they are happily married. Regardless of our apologies and the years that have passed, though, we realize a small wound is still present because of our words.

I can provide many examples of spouses who strongly dislike their in-laws. This type of difficult relationship is so prevalent it has become a cultural joke. This may seem like a radical observation, but I believe our support of marriage within our families will affect the divorce rate. Couples need support and love. Married individuals need to feel that their family members can love their partners almost as much they do. Even more, Jesus commanded it.

How can you support the marriages within your family?

- *Ask the Holy Spirit to help you analyze any bias toward the spouses of those in your family.*

  Have you passed judgment on an individual spouse? Many times, simply knowing we are operating from a place of judgment helps us treat this person with more respect.

Married individuals need
to feel that their family members
can love their partners almost
as much they do.

- *Ask the Holy Spirit to reveal any unforgiveness you have toward this person. Take the necessary steps to forgive.*

  Forgiveness will go a long way and help you as much or even more than it will help the other person.

- *Love and respect this family member's spouse.*

  Remember, this spouse is an extension of someone in your family. You have loved your family member for a long time, but your family member also chose this person for a spouse. This spouse has a place. Be part of the solution rather than part of the problem. Help your family member cultivate their marriage rather than attempt to break it apart.

WALKING WOUNDED

> His wounds became your healing. You were lost sheep
> with no idea who you were or where you were going.
> Now you're named and kept for good by the Shepherd
> of your souls
>
> —1 Peter 2:24b-25 MSG

Walking wounded. Doesn't that term describe almost all of us? I have yet to meet a person who doesn't have something in their past that has caused a wound. Consequently, most of us have faulty beliefs about ourselves. I am not trying to sound pessimistic—just realistic. We spend an excessive amount of time trying to pretend things are perfect, which keeps us from actually enjoying the good moments in this imperfect world. What would happen this Christmas if we made space for people, wounds and all? What if we created a place of safety rather than judgment?

Thankfully, I have people in my life who have created space for my "issues." They have allowed me to see a part of myself I never thought possible. They made room for me, all of me, even the wounds. They accepted me—even the broken, ugly, selfish, and guarded parts I vowed no one would ever see.

We spend an excessive amount of time trying to pretend things are perfect, which keeps us from actually enjoying the good moments in this imperfect world.

What would happen if we stopped to see the whole person this Christmas season? What would it be like if our families became the safest places rather than the places where we experience the most wounds? I know this is a tall order, but frankly, it's because you probably view this proposition from the perspective of your own wounds.

How can you help the walking wounded in your life?

- *Ask the Holy Spirit for revelation.*

  Every time I ask Him to show me someone—and I mean really show me—He does without fail. Ask Him to help you see *through* rather than see to—which means He will let you see beyond the surface of someone's life. The only time I am unable to see others and their wounds is when I let my own wounds and my desire to protect them take priority over seeing the truth.

- *Ask the Holy Spirit what wounds He wants to reveal and heal this Christmas season for you. He can, and He will.*

  Let me illustrate. Recently, I got a cut on my leg. I pulled out the antibiotic ointment and slapped on a bandage. The next day, I accidentally hit the same spot. Ouch! I thought I had forgotten about my injury, but one small bump was a quick reminder. This experience illustrates what many of us try to do with our emotional wounds; we use a bandage to cover them up and hope no one will bump them. But the holidays bring a plethora of scenarios to remind us of our wounds. How different would your life be if you took care of those wounds for the last time? Once the cut on my leg healed, I could bump it 20 times without any response. And you could come to the point where the most significant injuries you have endured no longer cause searing pain.

- *When the Holy Spirit gives you revelation about yourself and others, apply grace rather than judgment.*
  We are often the worst judges of ourselves. We shame ourselves for our imperfections. How silly is that? Stop trying to make yourself or your family perfect. Only Jesus is perfect, and He died so the rest of us don't have to be.

YOU ARE ENOUGH

> "What's the price of a pet canary? Some loose change, right? And God cares what happens to it even more than you do. He pays even greater attention to you, down to the last detail—even numbering the hairs on your head! So don't be intimidated by all this bully talk. You're worth more than a million canaries."
>
> —Matthew 10:29–31 MSG

You are enough. If you haven't heard someone say that to you in a while, take a moment now to pause and hear it. **You. Are. Enough.**

What is it about our families that sometimes makes us feel "less than"? We slip back into old behavior patterns we learned in childhood, which cause us to fall into "family norms" so quickly. Honorable men begin acting like boys, and distinguished women start behaving like girls. When you get to the root of the problem, you will find a need for acceptance and a feeling as if we are not enough. We take on old patterns to make up for *what we perceive* as a lack in our own lives. But listen again: you are enough. No other human has the power to define your worth.

In my own life, feelings of rejection are a "go to" for the enemy's attacks. He loves to convince me I will suffer rejection before an interaction even starts, and I find myself striving so hard to win acceptance from those around me. I fear they will reject me if I am not enough for them. Admittedly, this thinking is faulty, and I can see the destruction it has caused for me. It has convinced me to sacrifice more than I wanted to give, take more than I wanted to tolerate, and perpetuate a lie in my mind and behavior upon which the enemy feasts. But no more!

How can you deal with feelings of not being "enough"?

- *Get this phrase in your mind:* **I am enough.**

   Then don't let anyone or anything take it away. You are enough, no matter what you do, what you believe, or what other people perceive. Those around you do not define you. Why? Because God has already defined you, and through His Holy Spirit, He reminds you. I have yet to hear Him tell someone, "You are not enough."

- *Learn to see others as enough.*

   Other people are enough, regardless of what they do for you, say to you, or believe about themselves. Start the process of helping people recognize they are worthy rather than worthless. This message is crucial to the health of our families. We have to believe the best and allow others the opportunity to do the same.

- *Ask the Holy Spirit to reveal the areas of your life that make you susceptible to feeling "less than." Then be willing to listen and do something about it.*

   If the Holy Spirit tells you about a problem in your life, He won't simply make it go away. You have to do something about it. Take authority over the problem and eliminate it from your life.

You are enough. You deserve to feel that in every situation.

You are enough, no matter what you do, what you believe, or what other people perceive.

DOWN IN THE DUMPS

The sadness you have right now is similar to that pain, but the coming joy is also similar. When I see you again, you'll be full of joy, and it will be a joy no one can rob from you. You'll no longer be so full of questions.

—John 16:22-23 MSG

Depression is no joke. Ask those who have suffered from even mild depression, and they will tell you the same. Unfortunately, the Christmas season can bring out depression in all its dreary dread. Unmet expectations and unpleasant experiences make this struggle even more real to many.

Depression is not something of which anyone should be ashamed. Our culture often places a stigma on those who struggle with depression while elevating and honoring physical ailments. However, they are the same. We must counter our culture's views. We wouldn't fault a diabetic for not regulating their sugar levels, so why do we fault people who struggle with depression for not regulating their brain chemicals? It needs to stop.

The holidays can take on a life of their own. The Christmas season is full of parties, celebrations, and gatherings. When depression makes it difficult to get out of bed, putting on a party outfit is the last priority. If brushing your teeth feels like running a marathon, then sitting around a table with people you may not even like feels like a hike to Antarctica.

Find someone you can talk to. Whether you suffer from depression or know someone else who does, talk. Be there—make yourself available to someone. That person doesn't have to be a therapist unless the depression is severe. Then you most definitely need a mental health professional. But talking to someone is critical for dragging depression into the light and allowing the Holy Spirit to do something with it.

How can you address the matter of depression?

- *If you experience depression or know someone else who does, give grace!* You do not have to experience something to empathize and listen. Give yourself grace and don't buy into the cultural stereotype.
- *Drag these issues into the light and determine what is chemical and what is spiritual.* This advice may seem too simple, but if you need help differentiating what is what, then find a spirit-filled therapist to help you.
- *Sift your thoughts. Much of depression's nastiness will begin in your thought life.* Are you thinking about the holidays and trying to determine what you can't do or what you can? Are you thinking about what you're missing or what you have? Are you thinking about who you aren't or who you are? It only takes a single thought to take root and grow into a bigger belief.

Talking to someone is critical for dragging depression into the light and allowing the Holy Spirit to do something with it.

DUMP OUT YOUR PITCHER

> Don't fret or worry. Instead of worrying, pray. Let petitions and praises shape your worries into prayers, letting God know your concerns. Before you know it, a sense of God's wholeness, everything coming together for good, will come and settle you down. It's wonderful what happens when Christ displaces worry at the center of your life.
>
> —Philippians 4:6–7 MSG

Anxiety in my vocabulary is also known as *fear*. I find it creeps easily into my life during the holidays. I tend to stay on high alert and fret more at this time of year than any other. I think most of it is because I fear what others will do or say. Thinking about the actions of other people seems to be a trigger for me. I am always taking into account what others may or may not do. I call this experience *pre-worry*. I have the amazing ability to worry about something that may not even happen. You probably do too. Through pre-worry, I project my worry into the future as opposed to living in the moment. Because I'm multi-talented, I can also engage in worry in reverse (commonly known as *regret*). I am capable of sending worry into the past

Through pre-worry,
I project my worry
into the future as opposed
to living in the moment.

to engage with something that has already happened. Neither of these "talents" is a good or productive use of my time or yours.

When I speak with clients about anxiety, I imagine a pitcher of water and ask them to do the same. A person who struggles with anxiety is like a glass pitcher filled to the brim with water. You struggle and strain to carry it across the room without spilling a drop. When the pitcher is that full, anything life throws our way, such as finances, family, and friendships, only adds to the water level. Then it starts spilling over the sides. We then spend the majority of our time trying to collect the spilled water as opposed to dealing with what caused the spill in the first place. The goal in our lives, especially for those who struggle with anxiety, is to get our pitcher to halfway full. This new level allows room for any life stressors or things that may add to the daily struggles we encounter.

Many people can lower their water level by taking things off their plate; others may require medication. It all depends on the level of anxiety, how long it has been hanging around, and what it looks like for that individual. I always recommend talking to a mental health professional to distinguish what would be best for a particular person's version of anxiety and how to move forward with kicking it to the curb.

How can you better cope with anxiety?

- *Don't pre-worry or worry in reverse.*
  Neither of these are productive uses of your time, especially at this time of year when you have enough things pulling for your attention.
- *If you struggle with anxiety, talk to someone.*
  Talking helps you through your struggles and allows you to better determine what is worth the room in your pitcher and what isn't. Determine the type of person you will talk to. Do your worries warrant a talk with a friend or a professional? Let someone in to help you decide.

- *Ask the Holy Spirit to talk to you about the root of your fear.*
  He will reveal the source so you can then do something about it. People tend to overcomplicate finding the root and doing something with it. It really is as simple as hearing and being willing to look honestly at the source.

GRIEF

> There's more to come: We continue to shout our praise even when we're hemmed in with troubles, because we know how troubles can develop passionate patience in us, and how that patience in turn forges the tempered steel of virtue, keeping us alert for whatever God will do next. In alert expectancy such as this, we're never left feeling shortchanged. Quite the contrary—we can't round up enough containers to hold everything God generously pours into our lives through the Holy Spirit!
>
> —Romans 5:3-5 MSG

Grief. When we consider this word, we often think of the death or loss of a person we love. However, I have a therapist friend who taught me grieving is for more than just funerals. I understand the death of a loved one creates difficulty during the holidays. I feel deep compassion for those who have had this experience and find their grief amplified during this time of year.

However, grieving is something we must do for any circumstance or situation that does not turn out the way we thought it would. I could insert many of my holidays here. There are numerous things about which I have grieved or am grieving. I

Grieving is something we must do
for any circumstance or situation
that does not turn out the way
we thought it would.

thought these things would go a certain way, but they turned out vastly different. Sometimes I wish people would do more, be more, say more, or just make the smallest amount of effort possible. This loss requires grief. It requires me to pause and acknowledge the disappointment, sadness, and a myriad of other emotions. I have to let my heart feel these emotions and fully process them so they don't take permanent residence in my life. My simple act of grieving something that didn't go as planned allows me to operate from a position of forgiveness and freedom.

How can you deal with feelings of grief?

- *Stop and take some time.*
  Strangely enough, this is one of the most difficult things to do. It's not easy to allow ourselves to stop and lean into an emotion that isn't pretty, fun, or happy. However, it is essential if we want to move forward.
- *Acknowledge what didn't go the way you thought it would.*
  Whether you are concerned about how your pie turned out or the absence of one of your parents, remember that nothing is too small to grieve.
- *Do the work of letting it go.*
  This may mean trying again to make the pie or having a conversation with someone who was involved in a difficult circumstance. Either way, this work allows you to become free from the event. One of the most difficult things to do in these scenarios is allow yourself to come to terms with a permanent loss. If a parent didn't treat you well while you were growing up, or you had to rely on yourself more than you wanted to, moving forward requires the willingness and ability to accept it.

14

PACKING THE SUITCASE

In the original creation, God made male and female to be together. Because of this, a man leaves father and mother, and in marriage he becomes one flesh with a woman—no longer two individuals, but forming a new unity.

—Mark 10:6-8 MSG

In my opinion, one of the hardest holiday seasons is the first one after a couple gets married. Again, I'm stating my opinion. Some people probably call it their most magical, but it wasn't for me. The first Christmas together is usually difficult because the couple has to make many new decisions. *Where will we go? Whom will we see? What traditions will we keep, especially considering some of them may be quite sacred to us?*

When I think about all these decisions, a **suitcase** analogy comes to mind. When a couple marries, they both come with their own suitcases. One of the major goals and challenges of marriage is to get both individuals' "stuff" into one bag. The items in each person's suitcase are things held sacred—*by others for them*—rather than things they decide they need for themselves. Couples often discover something has been "packed" long after they've said, "I do." These extra things get thrown into the suitcases by family members and remain unseen until the couple tries to combine bags.

My husband and I took a great pre-marriage class. The class leaders shared an old story about a newly married couple cooking their first Christmas ham. As the two prepared to put the ham in the oven, the wife cut off the round end of the ham. The husband asked why she did it like that, and she replied, "That's how you make a ham." While discussing this ham preparation tradition with the wife's family members several days later, they made a discovery—the family cut off the end of the ham because the bride's grandmother did not have a pan large enough to fit the entire piece of meat.

Isn't that like so many things in our lives? We simply accept them as the way things are until we start asking questions. That bride believed all along that cutting off the round end was a required step for preparing a ham. In reality, her grandmother's necessity became a family norm until her husband asked her why. You will probably find a few things like this in your suitcase. Marriage gives someone with an outside point of view the opportunity to ask us why we have packed the specific contents of our suitcase. If we are willing to look with unbiased eyes, we might even save a serving or two of ham.

How can a couple address their separate and shared suitcases?

- *Evaluate what you have packed in your bag.*
  What did you personally pack? What did others pack for you? Which contents are necessary for moving forward in your life together? Ask why you feel that way. If you can successfully answer the why, you will find it much easier to put the right things in your shared bag.
- *Inevitably, you will find something that is difficult to leave behind, but your conscience and the Holy Spirit will let you know it needs to go.*

Marriage gives someone
with an outside point of view
the opportunity to ask us why
we have packed the specific contents
of our suitcase.

As a couple, seek out someone to help you find a resolution if this packing process creates a dilemma. You will need an objective person who can listen and understand you and your spouse. This person should be able to help you answer the why.

- *Decide what you will allow into the shared suitcase.*
  Remember, you can't pack ten outfits and only leave room for your partner to put in one pair of underwear and a toothbrush. Be fair. Divide the bag's space as equally as possible. The contents of your shared bag should allow both of you to "survive" into the future. If you carefully negotiate what is packed, you will not only survive but thrive as well.

MONEY

You're blessed when you meet Lady Wisdom,
  when you make friends with Madame Insight.
She's worth far more than money in the bank;
  her friendship is better than a big salary.
Her value exceeds all the trappings of wealth;
  nothing you could wish for holds a candle to her.
With one hand she gives long life,
  with the other she confers recognition.
Her manner is beautiful,
  her life wonderfully complete.
She's the very Tree of Life to those who embrace her.
  Hold her tight—and be blessed!

—Proverbs 3:13–18 MSG

"The love of money is the root of all kinds of evil" (1Timothy 6:10 NLT). The holidays can bring our full discomfort with this Scripture to life in a split second. **Money** always seems to become a topic of discussion between my husband and me during the holiday season. I am the type of Christmas shopper who never feels like we have "enough." I always feel as though we need to buy more for our family and friends. I also feel like I need to shower those I love with exorbitant amounts of baked goods, which as my mother so lovingly reminded me in middle school, do not come from ingredients the store gives away free.

Generosity can take on a life of its own and morph into something more for our own personal gain than for the people on the receiving end. Money in marriage requires agreement, or it will certainly create conflict. The stressors of the season are already out in full force; there's no need to add another. Healthy couples must be on the same page when it comes to money during the Christmas holidays.

How can you overcome struggles with money?

- *Set a budget.*
  I know, I know—no one likes that word (except perhaps accountants). Even so, if we don't tell our money where to go, it will take us to places we don't want to visit. Many individuals experience "the January jolt"—when the post-Christmas credit card statements come in the mail, bringing an overwhelming financial aftermath to all the holiday cheer. If you are married, talk to your spouse about your budget. If you aren't married, find a friend to talk to about where you plan to tell your money to go this holiday season. Our culture has made the discussion of money so taboo that we often struggle in silence. We don't want anyone to see the shocking reality of our bank account. This secret-keeping creates a culture of shame, guilt, and deception, none of which is healthy or productive.

- *Realize money doesn't always buy the things that matter.*
  Unhurried quality time with a friend or family member is more valuable than a store gift card you snagged at the last minute. We must start to define spiritual currency instead of putting so much emphasis on monetary things.

Generosity can take on a life of its own and morph into something more for our own personal gain than for the people on the receiving end.

BLENDED FAMILIES

> Anyone who neglects to care for family members in need repudiates the faith. That's worse than refusing to believe in the first place.
>
> —1 Timothy 5:8 MSG

Blended families comprise over 50 percent of the US population. I really dislike the ongoing stigma attached to this type of family, probably in large part because ours is a blended family. My husband was previously married and has a daughter. I have been a part of her life since she was two years old. She is a vital part of our— and my—family. I can't say I got to this point without some trial, tribulation, and frustration. Nonetheless, I am here now. This is our family, completely shame-free.

Christmas can present an extra level of difficulty when it comes to blended families. They deal with double the number (or more) of players, traditions, and wishes. This multiplicity is never easy to navigate, regardless of the level of your relationship. The holidays require a significant amount of grace, flexibility, and compromise. For many years, we did the "child exchange" on Christmas Eve or Christmas Day. It is never fun to watch a vital part of your family leave your celebrations to go somewhere else. One of the main lessons I've learned over the years of being a step-mom (or "bonus mom" as I like to say) is that honor is required. I must honor the other parent and her family regardless of my opinion. I have to engage my will in creating peace for my daughter, whether biological or not. This young lady deserves to celebrate and observe whatever traditions are on the other side of her family. Many parents spend too much effort trying to be "right" and "win." In the process, they fail to guard and steward the hearts of their children.

How can you support blended families?

- *Simply accept the fact stepfamilies exist.*
  They are part of our culture and here to stay. As much as we hope and pray for the success of all marriages, many will fail. We cannot perpetuate the misconception that a blended family isn't a family because of its origin. We have to be the change we want to see in our culture.

- *Ask the Holy Spirit to reveal your biases, inner vows, and places where you have dug in your heels.*
  Be honest with yourself. The more you attempt to cover up these issues and pretend they aren't there, the more dishonor you will give to your child.

- *Find opportunities to honor.*
  Regardless of your feelings, honoring others always wins. Honor is always best, and dishonor won't bring the change honor will.

Many parents spend too much effort trying to be "right" and "win." In the process, they fail to guard and steward the hearts of their children.

CHILDLIKE

> No prolonged infancies among us, please. We'll not tolerate babes in the woods, small children who are an easy mark for impostors. God wants us to grow up, to know the whole truth and tell it in love—like Christ in everything.
>
> —Ephesians 4:14–16 MSG

One of the most interesting observations I have made in my counseling career is watching CEOs of multi-billion-dollar companies turn into little boys at the thought of their parents. They can rule the boardroom, but they regress to family patterns in their own living rooms. My heart breaks for these individuals as well as others who have the same struggle.

One of the contributing factors to this **regression** is the inability of family members to put their own needs aside and lift up the greatness in others. Many individuals "need" the members of their family to regress so they can maintain a "reality," which keeps them in a place they feel safe, coupled with an inability to deal with their own issues.

This interplay is *co-dependency*. These interactions preserve a family system and keep it from evolving and becoming all it was meant to be. When members of a family do not have the freedom to be themselves because of anxiety, potential backlash, or possible repercussions, the system doesn't move at all. Individuals stay bound to their old patterns. This setup stinks, and it definitely isn't our best.

How can you address ongoing family patterns?

- *Be honest with yourself—you know when you do it.*
  You know when a familiar pattern comes calling; you fall right into the trap. Learn to recognize the situations in which you do not act like yourself.
- *Ask the Holy Spirit to reveal the reasons for your regression.*
  What is causing you fear? What would happen if you really acted like yourself? What price would you pay if you did what you normally would do and said what you normally would say? The answers to these questions will help you discover the motivation behind the why.
- *Do something about it.*
  You are not required to upend your family overnight; instead, try one small step toward being yourself when you gather with them. Stay true to the greatness within you. Lean into the work you have already done on yourself. Respect your past without letting it define who you must be today. Allow the past to inform your decisions, not make them for you.

Respect your past without letting it define who you must be today.

18

FAVORITISM

"Don't pervert justice. Don't show favoritism to either the poor or the great. Judge on the basis of what is right."

Leviticus 19:15 MSG

Favoritism means showing special favor. I admit this definition can make me cringe. I have experienced this issue in my own life and witnessed it in the lives of many of my clients. We struggle with favoritism because of our own desires to be enough, be seen, be loved, and matter. Sadly, these desires are often only met when we "perform." Have you noticed that much of favoritism is connected to behavior?

Favoritism requires a shift in power. Someone has to have authority over us and the power to make us feel "less than." I have much respect for authority and have seen how it can be quite beneficial; however, when it comes to my self-worth, only a few authorities can make me feel "less than." Many families, especially around the holidays, show favoritism in ways that define the self-worth of their members. Personally, I have spent many holidays battling this issue in my spirit. I have wrestled with thoughts of doing whatever I could to be whatever my family needed me to be so they would show me some favor.

We struggle with favoritism because of our own desires to be enough, be seen, be loved, and matter.

Fortunately, after many Christmas seasons, I have finally allowed myself to stop trying to gain approval. I have concluded that I am enough. I have decided that my performance shouldn't dictate the way others treat me. "Stuff" like gifts and money cannot make me feel worthy in the way true acceptance and time can. I have also decided that my family, especially my children, don't deserve to have the same wrestling match with favoritism in the future, and it is up to me to keep them away from it.

How can you deal with favoritism?

- *Admit to ourselves that favoritism and our "status" in our family does matter to us.*
  This can be a hard realization, but I have yet to find a person who doesn't wish their family would see them and accept them for who they are.
- *Investigate to whom we have given "false authority" and decide if they are really "worthy" of such a high honor.*
  This statement may be difficult to apply to your mother or grandfather, but we often allow blood relations to become a means of abusive behavior. Familial relations are never an excuse for someone to treat us in abusive or demeaning ways.
- *Evaluate the "exchange system."*
  What are we trading in exchange for time, money, gifts, or attention? Is that trade actually worth it? Most of the time, the answer is no.
- *Ask the Holy Spirit to affirm us in who we are.*
  The Holy Spirit can show us we are enough no matter what we do. He will provide for us, whether through a substitute parent to fill the void or extra gifts so the missing presents aren't even noticed. Allow Him to define you, and the rest will fall into place.

CONTROL

So, my very dear friends, when you see people reducing
God to something they can use or control, get out of their
company as fast as you can.

—1 Corinthians 10:14 MSG

Control. This word has such a powerful hold on so many people. I wish I could
tell you that I have no experience dancing with this villain, but unfortunately, I
do. Some significant events beyond my control happened in my childhood, one of
which was my mother's death during my toddler years. This traumatic event sent
me into a perpetual cycle of control. I could not control her death, but I would try to
control every other event possible. Unfortunately, the struggle for control manifests
pretty easily for me during the Christmas holidays. I find myself attempting to
control events, people, scenarios, and interactions to avoid hurt or abandonment.
I know my mom didn't intend to hurt or abandon me, but I was still left holding
those real emotions when she died. In the present, I have to work especially hard
during the holidays not to assume situations beyond my control will have the
same outcomes.

How can you overcome the issue of control?

- *Admit control is a coping skill.*
  I have to be honest with myself and make this admission. However, control isn't exclusive to my experience. I find most people have some level of struggle with control because they want to avoid feeling an unpleasant emotion or having an experience they dislike.
- *Tell someone else.*
  Simply being honest with myself isn't enough. I need to tell someone else, though this may feel like the last thing I want to do. Someone needs to have permission to tell us when we are acting a little "control freakish." We need a trusted person to call us out before our controlling behaviors take on a life of their own.
- *Ask the Holy Spirit to speak to you about your "why."*
  What is that thing inside you that makes you feel as though you *absolutely must* take control of a situation *or else*? Focus on the "or else" of the situation. What is really going to happen if you don't take control? Your answer will tell you exactly what is driving your desire to control. Our false "truths" are always dangerous behind the wheel, so don't let past events control you any longer. The ride is always better when the Holy Spirit drives.

We need a trusted person to call us out before our controlling behaviors take on a life of their own.

UPSETTING THE SYSTEM

One handful of peaceful repose
Is better than two fistfuls of worried work—
More spitting into the wind.

—Ecclesiastes 4:6 MSG

Systemic thinking is one of my favorite things to teach upcoming therapists. Significant power resides in naming and understanding the various systems with which we operate on a regular basis. The **family system** is the primary place we receive training about how to express emotion, follow social norms, and respond to the world. If the system is "broken" or full of maladaptive strategies, then this brokenness and these strategies are perpetuated generation after generation.

The holiday season presents us with an important choice. We have an opportunity to conform to the systemic norms or operate as our true selves. When individuals break away from family norms, it sends a disruption throughout the entire system, which can have either positive or negative effects. In my family, a few individuals tend to dictate the entire chain of events for our holidays. One year, I suddenly realized this structure existed, and I attempted to point it out. Needless to say, the system did not appreciate my newfound information nor my resolve not to engage in this systemic norm. Breaking away from established patterns requires courage, strength, and a lot of risk. I had to come to terms with the reality that the system may not shift with my revelations. Regardless of how others behave, though, I plan to operate from a position of truth.

How can you address flawed family systems?

- *Ask the Holy Spirit to reveal any "broken" or maladaptive strategies within your system.*
  You are likely already aware of most of them. These strategies are typically the things that feel weird and out of order when you compare your family to others.
- *Decide what you will do this holiday season or even another time of year.*
  Will you play by the "family norms" or create your own set of rules that the family system needs to understand?
- *Communicate any boundary or other matter with your family in a loving way.*
  Once you discover a dysfunctional family strategy, the temptation is to bulldoze your way through the holiday festivities, letting everybody know how they have been doing things the wrong way. This approach will never be productive without love. You cannot expect your family to change patterns that have taken years to establish just because you had a sudden epiphany. Lovingly share your concerns if you want to bring about lasting change.

Breaking away from established patterns requires bravery, strength, and a lot of risk.

NOT PICKING UP WHAT
THEY ARE PUTTING DOWN

Forget about deciding what's right for each other. Here's what you need to be concerned about: that you don't get in the way of someone else, making life more difficult than it already is.

—Romans 14:13 MSG

I love the phrase **"I am picking up what you are putting down."** I find myself saying it all the time when communicating to others that I understand exactly what they mean, whether they state it directly or imply it. However, this phrase can take a negative turn when it comes to family and the Christmas holidays. We often end up picking up what someone is putting down in a maladaptive way. We start to "take on" the issues of our family members or friends, and suddenly, their issues become our issues. *Don't do that.*

I really wish telling you not to do that was enough, but I frequently find myself in this situation as well. Other people's issues become my own—their anxieties, frustrations, and faulty coping strategies. This past holiday, I found I was trying to keep someone happy. I knew they had a specific issue, but they weren't willing

We start to take on the issues of
our family members or friends,
and suddenly, their issues
become our issues.

to talk about it. In an effort to keep them from having anxiety, I decided to own it for them—to take it upon myself. I decided to make things "easier" on them. As a result, I ended up working harder and giving that person permission to keep the issue as part of our holiday celebrations. I suppose I am scolding myself, but that's not very productive either.

How can you keep from "picking up what others are putting down"?

- *Separate **their** issues from **your** issues.*
  You will have to ask some hard questions. What is it that "they"—family, friends, or whoever—want you to own so they don't have to? This answer hurts and is hard to realize at times, but you can do it.
- *Find out how you can stay truer to what **you** need than what **they** need.*
  This process requires self-exploration and an honest look at the patterns of your family or friends. Looking at this stuff may be difficult at first, but you will find celebrating the holidays (or any other day) the way *you* want rather than how *they* want is so liberating!
- *Ask the Holy Spirit to help you not pick up what they are putting down.*
  Ask Him to help you know what to say and do so you can help them put their stuff down too.

YOU'RE NOT THE BOSS OF ME

Think of yourselves the way Christ Jesus thought of himself. He had equal status with God but didn't think so much of himself that he had to cling to the advantages of that status no matter what. Not at all. When the time came, he set aside the privileges of deity and took on the status of a slave, became *human*! Having become human, he stayed human. It was an incredibly humbling process. He didn't claim special privileges. Instead, he lived a selfless, obedient life and then died a selfless, obedient death—and the worst kind of death at that—a crucifixion.

—Philippians 2:6-8

This topic really hits close to home for me. It is something I have struggled with in my family for the entire duration of my marriage. For far too long I believed the lie that I had a faulty perception and that it wasn't as bad as I thought. But it wasn't my perception; it was reality. I have a person on either side of my family who is the "**monopolizer**." You know the person to whom I'm referring. This individual decides where we eat, how we do things, and if an event will go smoothly or not. You can imagine how annoying this is for other family members (like me), who have opinions too. I feel so frustrated when we are planning an event or activity, and the agreed upon plan suddenly changes because one person says so. I want to jump up and down and throw a tantrum.

The behavior creates a *hierarchy*. Anyone who knows me also knows I hate hierarchies. Anytime a person gets to dictate the group's schedule based upon their own desires, they are claiming a higher value or worth than everyone else. Without saying a word, they communicate a powerful message: "You are worthless, unheard, unseen, and devalued." And none of that is true. These behaviors become more pronounced during the holiday season since monopolizers have many opportunities to dominate family gatherings and celebrations.

How can you cope with monopolizers?

- *Explore whether or not there is a monopolizer in your family.*
  Can you identify that person? If you don't know already, ask the Holy Spirit to reveal the truth to you.
- *Set firm boundaries and don't allow them to be crossed.*
  Be flexible concerning insignificant issues but protect what matters most to you.
- *Have an honest conversation with the individual you have identified.*
  Give the monopolizer honest feedback about your feelings related to their ongoing behavior. Christmas dinner isn't the ideal time, but a loving yet firm conversation can go a long way.
- *Ask the Holy Spirit to be in it all.*
  Confrontations can be uncomfortable, but the Holy Spirit will always help you do and say the right thing.

Anytime a person gets to dictate the group's schedule based upon their own desires, they are claiming a higher value or worth than everyone else.

GETTING THE BLUES

Endings are better than beginnings.
Sticking to it is better than standing out.

—Ecclesiastes 7:8 MSG

This year I decided that Valentine's Day was going to start on January 4th, which was also the day I packed up my Christmas decorations. I know this is a bit early for Valentine's, but it is a way I found to combat the winter blues that sometimes set in when the Christmas season ends. I truly love the holidays. I am like a giddy school-girl as I walk down the aisles at my favorite department store on November 1st. Admittedly, I sometimes even help the employees unbox items because I can't wait to see the new tinsel and garland. I love the togetherness, warmth, and fun all the festivities bring to the season. I always struggle in January to find some excitement, as well as some decent sugar cookies.

I am not alone. Many people struggle with the **post-holiday blues**. We spend approximately two months packing our mantels and schedules with signs of the season, only to have it end with resolutions and kale. No wonder people feel a little bummed out. It's a real thing. I have to be aware of myself because I don't want to give the enemy any room to steal my intentionality as I peer into the next year.

I have to be aware of myself because I don't want to give the enemy any room to steal my intentionality as I peer into the next year.

I now those dates are only lines on a calendar, but they set the tone for the days, weeks, and months ahead. One of my closest friends loves January. Because of this fact, I can't understand how our friendship has survived sometimes. She loves the new and looking ahead to get a word from the Lord for the next year. She finds this experience invigorating. For me, I settle on the Valentine's Day décor.

How can you survive the post-holiday blues?

- *Recognize some things are in your control.*
  You decide whether to stay at home pouting because you had to put away the Nativity scene or to leave the house and do something fun. The "winter blues" become exacerbated by your diet, activity level, and sleep schedule. Many times, these things get way out of whack when the Christmas holidays end. Get these things in order because they are in your control.
- *Explore your true feelings about the holidays ending.*
  Was there something you didn't get to do? Did you do something you wish you hadn't? Did you want to do something differently? Evaluating and leaning into these things will give you the opportunity to make different choices in the future. This evaluation will also allow you to get in touch with how you are feeling so you will be able to get through it, rather than staying stuck in it.
- *Plan something—anything.*
  Plan a vacation, a party, or an outing. Plan a weekend of adventure. Significant research shows having something on the calendar to look forward to will give you the motivation to keep going. These new plans will provide you with a much needed boost of excitement for the days ahead, even though they won't be filled with casseroles and caroling. This year I decided to plan a Valentine's Day party for my friends. It was truly my coping strategy, but guess what? It worked.

CRAMMING

Don't waste your time on useless work, mere busywork, the barren pursuits of darkness. Expose these things for the sham they are. It's a scandal when people waste their lives on things they must do in the darkness where no one will see. Rip the cover off those frauds and see how attractive they look in the light of Christ.
Wake up from your sleep,
Climb out of your coffins;
Christ will show you the light!
So watch your step. Use your head. Make the most of every chance you get. These are desperate times!

Ephesians 5:11–16 MSG

Writing this book has truly been therapeutic for me. I hope reading it has been for you as well. It allowed me to shine a light on all my holiday issues. If it doesn't help you, at least feel comforted by the fact that it really helped me. I realize one of my biggest issues is **cramming**. My husband will second this motion—and maybe third or fourth. I love to maximize, and I believe this is a strength. But when I do it during the Christmas holidays, a lot of people can pay the price for the counterfeit manifestation of this gift. I love to see how much we can do and how much fun we can fit into one holiday season. This habit may sound good until you are spending the day running from place to place and at the end of said day have no idea if you even smiled once. I can become so focused on *doing* that I forget why I'm doing it and for whom I'm doing it. Cramming robs me and my family of the joy and fulfillment the activity was intended to bring.

With this revelation, I have corrected myself with the new goal to stay more in the moment. I am striving to create margin, which means I allow myself the opportunity to linger, mosey, and stay as long as I want. While slowing down isn't always possible, it definitely is a goal in as many situations as I can allow it. It keeps me from missing something great, which I would have overlooked while rushing to the next thing. Sometimes just seeing my younger daughter have a few moments to play or explore is worth the money, time, or effort it took to get there. If I rush to the next event, I am not allowing her—or me—a moment to find something new or fun. As I have been honest with myself, I've started asking the "why" behind the cramming. Asking hard questions isn't always easy or fun, but it is always helpful. I have discovered my belief that cramming everything in will make the situation perfect. What a lie! Perfection is a nonexistent destination on the map of our lives. There aren't any coordinates, and we waste so much time and energy trying to get there.

How can you slow down, enjoy each moment, and avoid cramming?

- *Do a tough evaluation of your schedule.*
  Discover what really works for your family and do your best to implement this schedule. For many people, myself included, a schedule can remove all opportunity to show the grace we and others need. Don't do this. Instead, make a schedule that allows margin, joy, and memories—not anxiety, rushing, and exhaustion.

I can become so focused on doing that I forget why I'm doing it and for whom I'm doing it.

- *Ask the Holy Spirit the "why."*
  What inside you makes you feel the need to rush to everything and every-where? To *what* are you running? And *from* what are you running? What are you trying to create? What memory are you trying to erase through doing something differently?
- *Make a list of events you would **like** to include this Christmas season.*
  Ask your family for input on how they want the holiday season to look. Take these suggestions and then examine the logistics. If three things fall on one weekend in December, rank them in the order of what will bring the most life to your family as a whole. Creating a calendar and priority list seems simple, but it will give you a needed visual for your days, weeks, and moments together.

SIFTING

> I'm not going to walk around on eggshells worrying about what small-minded people might say; I'm going to stride free and easy, knowing what our large-minded Master has already said. If I eat what is served to me, grateful to God for what is on the table, how can I worry about what someone will say? I thanked God for it and he blessed it!
>
> —1 Corinthians 10:29–30 MSG

Have you ever played in the sand? I think most people have. My brain often works in pictures, if you haven't noticed already. I envision a sand sifter, the kind that allows some grains to fall through the holes while bigger items like plastic army men or seashells stay at the top. I think this picture is particularly relevant when considering family and the Christmas holidays.

Often, we have a **"sifter"** with holes that are too big. As a result, we let every little emotion, action, and re-action come through and affect us. God designed us for the junk like sand to sift through and leave the good, the fun, and the valuable on top. However, we allow others' perceptions and negative responses to remain

God designed us for the junk like sand to sift through and leave the good, the fun, and the valuable on top.

at the top. This problem is especially pronounced during the Christmas season. At this time of year, others' ideas and judgments seem to hold even more value than normal. Many people experience wounds from their family or friends by taking something too personally or misconstruing the intent of a message. Their "sifter" allows negative thoughts and responses to take root in their hearts, ruining their holiday joy.

How can you improve your "sifter"?

- *Consider some of the unpleasant scenarios.*
  Were there times when you found yourself offended by a family member or took on the "junk" dished out by a friend? Analyze these events. Is there a theme? Was there any merit to what you let through your sifter? Or was it something you should have let fall through like grains of sand?
- *Let the Holy Spirit speak to those situations, especially if you see a theme.*
  If you see a theme, there is typically a root. The same type of offense will likely keep hounding you until you address it.
- *Give yourself some grace.*
  I don't intend for this exercise to bring you shame or guilt. My goal is to allow you to own your joy, fun, and thoughts while allowing the issues of others to fall through like tiny grains of sand.

CONCLUSION

You made it! You made it through the stories, your own memories, and the difficult questions that may have made you want to punch me in the face at times. Whether you read one chapter or the whole book, I am praying you have a little bit more **hope**—hope that you are strong and can overcome this holiday season and many to come. I am praying hope is something you can tangibly cling to during the times in your life, specifically the holiday season, when you feel like you are the only one seeing things the way you do (especially when your Aunt Edna makes you feel crazy).

I know you have **courage**. You made it to this part of the book. In my opinion, asking the Holy Spirit even one of those questions is difficult, let alone all of them. I find that many individuals don't ask the Holy Spirit the tough questions because they are afraid of the process. However, after many years of counseling, I can testify that He is kind, loving, and eager to make things easy. I am so proud of your courage, and I am confident you are better for it.

Lastly, I cannot wait to hear stories of your **gumption** (cassie@cassiereid.com). Setting healthy boundaries and taking care of ourselves can be hard (I include myself in this), but we are so worth it. I can't wait to hear the stories of you "taking back" your holidays, making healthy memories with your family, and discovering the joy that was always meant to be at the center of this season. Know you are not alone. Many others are right there with you, myself include. May each new year bring a merrier Christmas and a happier holiday season to us all.

ABOUT THE AUTHOR

Cassie Reid, PhD, LCP-S, is the director of the Master of Marriage & Family Therapy graduate degree program at The King's University. She developed and launched this program in 2016. In 2010, she founded Cassie Reid Counseling, a practice where she leads a team of licensed professional counselors and licensed psychologists who use spiritual freedom, learned therapy, and a variety of other techniques to provide clients with powerful plans to combat any problems they face.

Dr. Reid's professional service also includes serving as a school counselor and special educator in a North Texas school district, interning at the University of Texas Southwestern Medical Center, managing the Texas Woman's University Counseling and Family Therapy Clinic, working as a member of the National Institute of Health research grant in pain management, partnering with numerous grief organizations, and serving as a Texas Licensed Professional Counselor Supervisor for over 30 counseling interns. This experience, together with Dr. Reid's skill and approachability, equip her to provide clients with counseling and therapy best suited to their needs.

Dr. Reid received a PhD in Marriage and Family Therapy from Texas Woman's University in Denton, TX, an MA in Educational Counseling from Texas Christian

University in Fort Worth, TX, and a BA in Psychology from Bethany College in Bethany, WV. She and her husband, James, actively serve at Gateway Church in the Dallas/Fort Worth Metroplex. One of their greatest joys is parenting their two daughters, Londi and Emerson.